Glass Awash

Poems by Ken Gierke

Spartan
Press

Spartan Press
Kansas City, Missouri
spartanpresskc.com

Acknowledgments:

Special thanks go to the editors of the following publications where these poems first appeared:

Pain & Renewal, edited by Brian Geiger: "unwound"

easing the edges: a collection of everyday miracles, edited by d.ellis phelps:"Linear Freedom" and "The Intent of Moonlight and Ethereal Synapses"

The Ekphrastic Review: "Ageless"

Additional thanks go to Jason Ryberg, John Dorsey, and Jon Freeland for their encouragement and support, and special thanks to Robert Okaji for his advice in the early stages of this collection.

Table of Contents

Even burnished glass will retain its luster

when viewed in the proper light.

So it is with memories.

This book is dedicated to my parents, Rudy and Donna Gierke, who are always in my thoughts, and to Bonnie Close, who is both my muse and my tsunami.

Words without Voice

How do I reconcile
      thoughts as fantasy
            memory and reality
      passion with voice
the page as desire?

vision disjointed

      no oracle

         writer

      thoughts recede

         fade

empty page

Wrestlution

I walk these paths
life's threads, often tangled
beyond recognition

finding what matters
most, resolution
no simple matter

destinations
beset by vexations
complications, estimations
taking stock of situations
convoluted permutations
constant need of calibration
source of endless consternation

I wrestle with knots

Slow Descent into Darkness

I search for answers and wonder, would I recognize them?

How can less be known, the more that is revealed?
Perspective tarnishes the truth.

What is my worth among the plight of others?
Who decides?

This person, but not another?
Chance robs even the worthy.

Does hardship serve a purpose?
A thousand butterflies cannot carry the world.

Why give more, when destiny delivers less?
What is hunger to a dying man?

Is there futility in standing firm,
when time holds all power?
Is life anything more than a footnote?

Why do we accept events as destiny,
and not a matter of chance?
A lightning strike means nothing to a burning forest.

Of what value are answers revealed, when no longer needed?

A lesson still holds true when learned too late.

Does strength hide in the slow descent?

.

Drought in the Depth of Marianas

Inundation is just the beginning.

The sea would walk
and with it take the shore.

Canyons deep hold secrets
never known, never told.

Truths never to be taken back
once exposed.

Bleached coral will not be
the only sign of lost innocence.

A parched tongue
has no way to hold words.

A drought of imagination
leaves little hope of recovery.

Out of Touch

I thought of the future, and spoke of the past.

-Truman Capote, *Breakfast at Tiffany's*

Through a haze that erases
possession and masks potential,
where is the horizon?

I grasp but find nothing.
There is no satisfaction
in what is denied.

Past and future out of reach,
the present slips away
with each passing moment.

Hollow Man

faint memory

arms wide open
embracing all held dear

hands now lifeless
at his sides

gut hollowed

little left to his frame,
once standing tall

fading into nothingness

Reaching

There is a way out of this darkness.

I touch it.

Feel it.

But I cannot grasp it.

The ever-changing veil that separates
us makes me wonder…

Am I reaching into the darkness?

In Search of Clarity

Through shifting circumstance
I walk a maze in darkness

Every day less certain
of a light that eludes me

Wondering if the next turn
will bring the answer

When each question builds new walls

bridge

rusting hulk
immersed in traditions
long abandoned

refusing to succumb
yet mindlessly adrift
in stagnant currents

what toll
to cross this bridge
pulling me down?

unwound

hope
a lie lost in fragments, scattered
like bits of a broken shell

misery
a watch left unwound,
merely witnessing time

defeat
grief anticipated,
fulfilled by default

overturned, untended,
a boat left to the elements
will not hold a net,
fish another day

cinder and ash

flames in a frenzy
unlimited resolve
with no restraints

reaching, stroking
caressing
a barrier against the cold

dancing, flickering
grasping at possibilities
among the embers

all of that and more
together in love
now, just a memory

wasted, scattered
by careless steps
cinder and ash

driftwood

a caress, like driftwood
slowly turning in its eddy

my waves lapping your shore

the ebb and flow
within your bay

intimate, yet never fully
embraced

Tinnitus

The hiss of breaking
foam, the last trace
of a receding wave.

The scale of monotones
at the bottom of a trough
offers no horizon.

Drowning in the crashing
of the next wave
and the next.

No walk along sandy shores,
the feel of lapping waves.
Oppression testing

resilience. Fighting to rise
above the undertow
that's all in my head.

Polarized

A filter around my heart
too long to remember
blinds me to truth I would deny.

Removed, it reveals a rift
too wide to bridge consuming
the love meant to consume us.

We've become
wave shimmers,
never-touching points of light.

Propensity

Missives in verse
expressing hope

The words reflected in a lover's eyes.

Confirmation sought
Love laid bare

Seeing only what he wants to see.

Easier than accepting
futility
paddling upstream in rapids

A wound that swallows words whole.

The past imagined
unravels

Some memories are best left for others.

Stranded

No infinite plane, this life
The far edge closer than the beginning

Options fewer than yesterday
Fewer than fear will allow

No course set in a mind
looking back for direction

My Road Not Taken

each path a conundrum
intersections unmarked
each fork a temptation

blind corners
dead ends hidden
in an unmapped maze
with no view of the horizon

all the hallmarks of Fate

Empty Canvas

An artist relates views seen
through the mind's eye, with no guarantee
his message to the world can be easily seen.

Painting a picture does not make it so.

The same may be said for the words on a page.
What of a man whose words bring no recognition,
no bolt from above?

Should poet and painter lay down brush and pen,
never give fruit to their visions?
Does a sunset lose its beauty if all are blind?

Though it may be sad if the world is unaware
of their work or just doesn't care,
neither painter nor poet welcomes this dream:

No word or brushstroke for their eyes to see.

Mantle

Always overlapping, touching
at times, the distance between
your world and mine grows

shorter as the seasons pass.
Serenaded by crickets,
we poke the embers,

while fireflies deliver
a semaphore yet to be decoded.
Your time no longer long,

mine not as short, your example
the lesson that will guide me
through your coming absence.

Long Term Short

Hidden
in the pockets of my mother's dreams,
surrounded
by the accumulated lint
of a faded lifetime, are dusty memories
sharper
than this morning's breakfast.

When her eyes close
one final time, will her last vision
be of those gathered around
or of those who've peopled her dreams?

Frailty

Cold, her hand in mine,
as I watch her fluttering eyes,
barely register her shallow breaths.

Shards of silence slice my heart,
skewering all sense of security
planted there in my youth.

That I am seen as the strength
to carry us through this end,
her final season, makes it no easier.

An occasional whimper slips through
her curtain of sleep induced by medication,
deepening those wounds, sapping any strength

from this mantle I've worn since his death,
when all I want is to be the child,
her hand holding mine.

Asleep with Grieg

Notes from Grieg's piano concerto weave
through my sleep to reveal a table in dim light
surrounded by darkness. An aged porcelain bowl
holds broth shimmering from silver to gold,
notes floating from its surface. Passing
from my spoon to her lips, they spread
throughout her body. My eyes open
as Grieg's notes fade.

His music resumes as my slumbers return.
I am sitting at her bedside, stroking her hand
to sooth her worries. Peace flows through her
and back into me. My concern for her is eased
as I wake to the last notes of Morning Mood.

Returning notes lull me into sleep
as dawn's light is filtered through
a sheer curtain in a dark-paneled room.
The shadowed mood is accented
by the light of a table lamp
beside my overstuffed, green velvet chair.
Tassels on the cream colored shade rustle
as I reach for a gilded letter opener
lying on the table. As the somber notes of
The Death of Ase sound, the blade raises
to my neck. A barely perceptible line appears.

One small drop of blood falls to the floor
bringing life and light to the room
with the sounds of Anitra's Dance.

Heavy Heart

Sometimes the great bones of my life seem so heavy

Mary Oliver, Spring Azures

He left much earlier than anyone expected,
succumbing to the ravages of an illness
that had plagued his life, the last six months
the hardest. For him. For us.

Our assurances could never replace him.
And so she went on, happy for family
while missing their life together,
missing his love for fifteen years.

Holding her hand, I sit beside her bed.
Family photos on the wall of this small room
speak louder than the words that leave her lips.
How long do I need to stay here?

Speaking softly, I tell her it won't be long.
She will be with him, at last.
Together but gone, both of them.
No night could be heavier than this.

Torrents

Wrapped in the roar of the cataract,
you stood with a swaddled bundle
brought to witness the strength
of a mighty force of nature.
Held close to your breast,
winter's ice could not invade
the warmth that surrounded me,
a strength that has been
steadfast to this day,
yet has now begun to fade.

Wishing that I could hold you
close to my own breast
on this darkest of nights,
I am pummeled by a waterfall,
emotions that would drown me
if not for the strength
you have instilled in me.

Desire for Genius

Towering
like a darkened flame,
a cypress bridges earth to sky.

A chaotic whorl of stars,
brilliant only in the dark of night,
struggles to rival the moon's crescent.

Windowed lights offer comfort
to those within, relief
from encroaching darkness.

Brushstrokes beckon the eye.
Follow Vincent's lead,
a master's inspiration.

If my pen followed his brush,
would lines lead to the brilliance
of darkness or that of light?

One Tear

Within the curve of this
well of my grief
lie memories of a life.
Merging.
Flowing.
Cleansing.
Giving strength greater
than taken.

Within this one tear
lie memories of a life,
yet no one tear
falls alone.

Visions of Absence

In darkness filled with the light of memories,
I call out in a voice that carries no weight.
The silence of your response echoes
in scenes that play out before me,
moments always out of reach but never
far from my mind, even in waking dreams
when I know you are gone but always
with me. Separation knows no distance.
Dreaming or awake, day and night
are the same, your absence all the difference.

View from the Bottom of a Well

The cloud of what-ifs
and why-nots

hanging over me
dizzies my mind

while the blue expanse
threatening to break

the hold of that ceiling
shielding my despair

offers no freedom
from those questions.

Inclinations

Who can tell a lawn
to be a lawn, tell water
not to flow

downhill?

Grass does not discern
between drought and soil
washed away,

conceding

to conditions a fawnlily
willingly accepts.
Where one fails

to cover,

the other heals,
as water continues
to flow,

or fails to fall.

Driving with Miles

(random riffs on the road)

Rain falls, steady, and I say so what.
Wipers try in vain to keep the beat,
but this combo is too tight.
The bass just layin' it down,
horn and sax sparring.

There's a fog rolling through the hills,
tellin' the rain
hold the ice, this is just too cool.

Bare branches, with pines the only green
in a landscape of white on brown.

Wait!
A lone birch like a ghost that knows.
As blue as this feels,
there will be no blue sky.

And that so what refrain slips in
and out.

Narrow roads now,
winding through wet grass
lined with granite and marble.

A memorial among memorials,
some barely legible.
Everything here is blue,

except the pines, white now with big, heavy flakes.
Country roads skirt the mountains.
Snow now a powder hangs in the air
like a fog. Roads slicker than the music.

Hands tense on the wheel.
Piano eases through me, slowly
levels out, brings me back to the lake,
out there somewhere,
blue asleep within the white.

Untapped

Stunted stalks cling
to a plot, parched
and windblown.

Like tears denied,
a cistern lies
empty.

With rain comes balance,
and healing begins.
Welcome tears.

Winter Garden, Spring's Promise

Fractals on a winter pane map the choices
I face, the surreal landscape of emotions
silently sculpted in a long night of loss

barely discernible in its blanket of grief.
Memory, the breeze that wends its way
through my soul, carries soft echoes of the pain.

The changes wrought by winter welcome
new growth. Fractals shift, offer a glimpse
of a garden waiting for spring,

its colorful promise mine to keep.
Joyful, like the seasons I knew
before that long winter.

Decompression

Horizon drained of life, water just as dull.
Boat rising, falling on whitecap accents.

Hand firm on mask of concession,
falling back into grayness.

Descending on a line leading
to remnants of a life consumed.

Light slicing layers of darkness,
baring bones of wasted wreckage.

Surveying remains bearing the weight
of experience in monotones.

Writing words in silt does nothing to alter history.
Turn to return. Minimal light expands on ascent.

Past left behind. In a world not so gray,
surface sheen a welcoming sight.

Adagio for Strings

One heart stops, while another beats,

yet feels as though it has stopped,
knowing that mourning
has the power to be endless.

Time passes, and a life follows
its course, its pulse subject
to random intrusions.

Music will play the strings
of a heart, so that it seems
as if it will never heal.

A memory, no true intrusion,
may become a knife, turning,
tracing old scars.

Yet it's the brilliance of that music
and the beauty of those memories
that have the power to sustain.

A heart continues to beat.

Stars Overhead

Even on a night
blacker than any other,

a light is repeated
to infinity.

Beauty that mirrors life.
Simple, yet complex.

Comfort in the stars.

Once Broken, Healed

The world breaks everyone, and afterward,
some are strong at the broken places.

-Ernest Hemingway, *A Farewell to Arms*

What is loss but an empty space,
that which waits to be filled?

The generation that was last
at the time of your passing,
was not the last.

That which follows holds a place
of its own that encompasses
what once was, always will be,
you, knowing all that you were
and all that you held.

Ruby-throated Fondness

Hazel eyes, always
dancing, even in age-
slowed years, transient

after transient, accumulated.
Reperfusion, less
effective with each

occurrence. Thoughts'
movement scattered
in consistency.

Distant past, light
gone, not forgotten,
hazel dances

in my mind, triggered
by a thought, a word,
a sight to spin

their sparkle across
the floor of
my mind.

A hummingbird hovers at the feeder.

On Holding Nothing

Behind me, decades.
Around me, the same.
Past and present as one.

Something a long time coming
does not bring acceptance
in the blink of an eye.

Harmony can be deceptive.
The underlying discord
woven through ours
for those same decades
was easier to dismiss
than to face head on.

Holding on to something
that was long gone,
I wandered, lonely
as a cloud in skies
that held only darkness.

When I realized the darkness
was behind me, the decades
slipped away, revealing blue skies.

Out of the Eddy

Drawn by avoidance,
the peril of drifting,
rudderless, becomes too real.

The current guiding me
resists, and possibilities unfold.

Elusive

Wary of your touch, it will recede,
parting like a fog, revealing nothing.

What is enlightenment, when what you seek
is the very nature of the haze?

Gently gathering what you can,
draw it into you. You are wary now,

knowing that to smother it will lead
to loss. As an early morning dew

would embrace the gossamer
of a delicate web, you feel its texture,

searching for reason, signs of truth.
It flees as you wake, and you wonder

just what it was you held. Stray thoughts,
lost to sleep, never reach the page,
nor fall on any ear.

Visions of Slumber

Thoughts ripple through me,
the wave of the past day washing over me.

This place knows me well. Troubles scatter
at its 300-thread count caress. Dreams
fold onto each other, struggle to take hold.

Fantasies caress me, illusion
woven with the familiar. Immersion
in each moment an eternity,
until I surface to breathe.

Individual details become indiscernible.
Lost within a ringing ear, the hum of the furnace.
One eye opens, almost expecting
to glimpse what's already faded away.

Change bordering on sanity trips
my synapses as thoughts shudder.

The light of my clock, stark
in the darkness swallowing it,
chews at the confines enveloping me.

I rise to the cold floor of reality.

Receding Waters

We walk
a brick-lined street, rainwater

flowing here,
turning there, lightning flashes

illuminating
the course of our lives

in freeze frames, the choices
faced, decisions avoided,

waiting for the sky to clear.

Vantage

The cold iron
that anchors me to my years
I bear without regret.

Though it has compounded
through mishap, trial,
and grief, I yield not to that weight.

That experience has brought me here.
I embrace it as my own.

Tsunami

Stagnant emotions divested,
detritus left by a receding tide.

Complaisance abandoned,
no longer rudderless.

Alternative considered.
Landlocked not an option.

Contact desired, a remedy
for the loneliness of being adrift.

Connection made in the warm embrace
of a welcoming harbor.

No destruction, here, but the ensuing
tsunami engulfs my senses.

Potential

Cornflower, pale
at first glance, seems
royal blue against
a barn's weathered gray.

Scheherazade, soft
and muted, rises to a crescendo,
Nikolai's vision dancing
in your mind.

Lips brush the cheek of a child
or an elder with comfort
and respect, yet become sensuous
in a lover's embrace.

Vanilla on the tongue
squanders its aroma,
teasing the palate until it
finally swims in sweetness,

refined and tapped,
overwhelming.

Into the Blue

Floating at ease

seventy feet down

twenty feet above

a tropical reef

I am my surroundings

As I am in the Blue

the Blue is in me

and as I leave

it stays with me

A threshold to cross

like a plane

not an ascension

nor a transcendence

a place within

Blue, as it is

on first entering

deep, in all ways

with no bounds

Always, until it is not

as my mind slips back

to the now

that is always here

Distractions

may mask the Blue

calling to my senses

But once it drifts through

contentment surrounds

the here of the now

dulling its edges

as I slide

...Into the Blue

Stone to Flesh

Gather the darkness in these chambers,
flowing from one to the next.
Banish it. Winter has lived here too long.

Be my salvation. Know these walls were
not always stone. They have moved
with each beat, known the fire of love.

Ear to my chest, hear the surge
you bring, stampeding horses
rushing to meet you, greet you.

As moon transitions, crescent to full,
so too these chambers, your touch
shifting stone to loving flesh.

Other Voices

The solitude blowing off
the water will stretch the truth of this,
as it replies to words meant only for you.

Sifting your fingers through stones
at the water's edge, trying to find
that one that speaks to you, do you know

it will look like all the others, once it dries
and the wind has taken its voice? Gather
its companions, stir them

in your hand, hear them speak. Know
there are others who have walked this path,
played this scene in their minds.

Thoughts without Voice

Noodles, instead of rice.
Does that recipe call for ginger or turmeric?

Climbing the backyard hill hurts her hips.
It's time for a visit to the vet.

You can have your equal rights.
Just don't deny their right to deny them.

Rain is predicted for this weekend.
I should take the kayak out today.

That pension cut is going to make things tight.
Fuel points for buying groceries. The logic escapes me.

A winter without snow. Go figure.
I need new tires before next winter.

Fixed in place for forty years, the mortar turned to dust.
This time, a dovetail. In all respects.

Wave the flag and close the borders.
Has anyone thought of that?

Linear Freedom

Somewhere beyond
the lines that separate us,
outside the angles they form,
beneath the layers
and complexities they create,
lies the course of a line
that we imagine, one
that erases all other lines.

A simple curve. A circle,
yet free from restraint,
that enables us to escape
those layers and complexities
that stifle us, as we imagine
a better place. One that
excludes none and holds all.

Glass Awash

Edges smooth,
rolling, tumbling.
Luster restored

in the wash
of a lapping blue,
kissing the sand

as it rises, falls
with each wave.
Tumbling again

and again, nudged
finally to lie
beneath the drying sun.

From swaying reeds,
a red-wing remarks on
its beauty, soon consumed

by a frost, a reminder
of each kiss found
in grains of sand.

Out of the Rain

He wades through dusk,
loss pelting him,
when she approaches

like dawn with its dew,
a touch bringing
a true rain.

Clouds retreat, revealing
light as they part,
forgotten colors

once abandoned,
returned
to his waking gaze.

The Intent of Moonlight and Ethereal Synapses

A haze struggles to dim a light traveling
the distance that binds two bodies.

Our growing world of disconnect, challenged
by invisible connections. Clouds shift,

strain to cast shadows, oblivious to the aura
framing them. Different wavelengths of light,

thoughts conflicting, gelling. Powerless
to impede, branches sway their hips to its pull,

the flow from one chamber to the next echoing
tidal forces, defying the disconnect, absorbing

those wavelengths in a way not imagined
but realized. The embrace of affirmation, a kiss.

tangible

a thought, passing
from one to another

and back

to them, tangible within
senses heightened by its presence

recognized, without a trace
of doubt by those who know

love

Solace for Theseus

Even daylight can fail.
Unexpected turns, a dark passage
leading to one closed door.

Opened
to a landscape shifting
with each breath taken.

A winter plain, starker
than any waste. Your kiss
on my cheek, its soothing warmth.

Confined in a desert canyon,
your touch a healing salve
against an unforgiving sun.

Under darkened skies, your eyes
blazing the way, unraveling
the thread of this labyrinth.

True Love

No mountain lake mist,
gone with the rising sun.

Nor melting snow of spring.

Not the silence of a stream in drought.

Nor the unattainable hope of a desert vision.

A mountaintop, crown glistening above the clouds.

A cardinal and its mate feeding, beak-to-beak.

Knowing joy by your side.

Memory's Stones

senseless order arranged
by each receding wave

stones with the fresh-minted
look granted by water and light

dulled with each breath
taken, new order imposed

by the next wave
and the next

thoughts jumbled
memory just a memory

Wide Awake?

Eyes open,
we conjure visions
to soothe us
in our sleep,

while around us
dreams wait to unfold
next year,
tomorrow.

Now.

The Journey

write of hope,
survival, like a flame
to have mattered is a joy

become a better vessel
let go of illusions
learn how to say goodbye

tomorrow is an uncertainty
brought into manifestation
the fruits of our learning

separation through loss
or death is illusion
see both sides of life

choose the way forward
dare to dream
love life

Living for Now, and Then

Don't look back.
The voice of my past
telling me to move on.

There's nothing to see here.
But there was.
There are stories

I have to tell you before
they are lost. Lessons learned.
Experience is for the inexperienced.

I was. I am, still. Just
as you are, will be.
Live for today, but remember.

If you learn anything from this,
and you will, remind yourself
of that. You will be thankful.

Ageless

I hold a voice, sometimes
feel it slip between my fingers.

Grasp a little tighter. Not so tight
as to startle it or send it fleeting.

Just enough to let it know
I remember, understand

its time is not limited to my past,
its confusion a sign I have more to learn.

Its wonder reminds me to be open
to possibilities, that even decay

and loss can lead to growth.
I hold that voice to my ear,

remember
beginnings never really end.

Ken Gierke is a retired truck driver, transplanted to Missouri from Western New York. After only ten years here, he is actually coming to think of Missouri as home, in spite of muddy water and a dearth of maple trees. While his poetry has appeared in several anthologies, this is his first published collection.

This project was made possible, in part, by generous support from the Osage Arts Community.

Osage Arts Community provides temporary time, space and support for the creation of new artistic works in a retreat format, serving creative people of all kinds — visual artists, composers, poets, fiction and nonfiction writers. Located on a 152-acre farm in an isolated rural mountainside setting in Central Missouri and bordered by ¾ of a mile of the Gasconade River, OAC provides residencies to those working alone, as well as welcoming collaborative teams, offering living space and workspace in a country environment to emerging and mid-career artists. For more information, visit us at www.osageac.org

Osage Arts Community

Lightning Source UK Ltd.
Milton Keynes UK
UKHW012025231222
414414UK00007B/56